Money Mindet: Frugality Unleashed

30 Days to Financial Independence and a Life of Abundance

Lulu Bell

Contents

Chapter One

Introduction to Frugal Living

The Benefits of Frugal Living

L iving a frugal lifestyle may seem daunting or even restrictive to some, but the truth Is that embracing frugality can lead to numerous benefits that extend well beyond financial gains. In this book we will explore the advantages of frugal living and how it can contribute to your journey towards financial independence and a life of abundance.

One of the most obvious benefits of adopting a frugal lifestyle is the positive impact it has on your finances. By practicing mindful spending and making conscious choices about how you allocate your resources, you can save substantial amounts of money. This newfound financial stability opens up a world of opportunities, allowing you to pay off debt, build an emergency fund, or invest in your future.

Frugality also encourages resourcefulness and creativity. When you embrace a more minimalist approach to life, you begin to question your actual needs versus wants. This shift in mindset prompts you to find alternative ways to meet your needs without overspending. You may discover the joy of repurposing items, finding hidden gems at thrift stores, or even cultivating a DIY mentality. Not only does this foster a sense of self-sufficiency, but it also promotes a greener and more sustainable way of living.

Moreover, frugal living can positively impact your mental and emotional well-being. By detaching yourself from the consumerist mindset, you free yourself from the constant pursuit of material possessions. Instead, you focus on experiences, relationships, and personal growth. This shift in priorities often leads to greater contentment, reduced stress, and increased happiness. As you become less reliant on external validation through material possessions, you find fulfillment in the simple joys of life.

Frugality also aligns perfectly with the Financial Independence, Retire Early (FIRE) movement. By adopting a frugal lifestyle, you can accelerate your journey towards financial independence. The more you save and invest, the quicker you can reach a point where you have enough passive income to sustain your desired lifestyle, giving you the freedom to retire early or pursue your passions without worrying about financial constraints. Keep in mind much of our work around frugality will be mindset adjustment. Frugality doesn't mean going without, it is more about reevaluating what means the most to you.

Frugal living offers a plethora of benefits that extend far beyond monetary gains. By embracing a frugal mindset, you can cultivate financial stability, resourcefulness, sustainability, and emotional well-being. Whether you are looking to improve your finances, reduce your environmental footprint, or simply find greater contentment in life, frugality can be a transformative practice that leads to a life of abundance and fulfillment.

Understanding Financial Independence and the FIRE Movement

Financial independence is a concept that has gained significant popularity and traction in recent years. It refers to the ability to live off your savings and investments without the need for a traditional job or a steady income stream. Achieving financial independence empowers individuals to have more control over their time, pursue their passions, and live life on their own terms.

The underlying principle of the FIRE movement is simple: save a significant portion of your income by adopting a frugal lifestyle and invest those savings wisely to generate passive income. It emphasizes the importance of living below your means, cutting unnecessary expenses, and prioritizing long-term financial goals over short-term gratification. FIRE has many variations depending on life goals and resources. People's FIRE plan may be Fat FIRE -a more easygoing attempt to save more while giving up less. Lean FIRE which is a stricter devotion to minimalist living. Barista FIRE, which is for those who want to quit the nine-to-five rat race and are willing to cut back their spending while working only part-time to do so.

Some important areas to consider when developing your own financial freedom plan for a life of abundance involve

1. Defining financial independence: Delve into the concept of financial independence, exploring its benefits and why it has become so desirable in today's society and work out where this sits with your own hopes and dreams.

2. The pillars of financial independence: Key principles that form the foundation of financial independence, such as frugality, saving, investing, and passive income generation.

3. Building a frugal lifestyle: We will guide you through the key components of a 30-day frugal living challenge, providing practical tips and strategies to reduce your expenses and increase your savings. You can then decide which parts of a 30-day challenge will be on your first go. Hopefully incorporating some 30-day challenges into your regular life throughout the year on your path to financial freedom. This frugal challenge will help you develop the necessary habits to achieve financial independence.

Reading is a great way to ensure you are equipped with the knowledge and tools to embark on your own journey towards financial freedom, ensuring a life of abundance and self-empowerment. Remember, financial independence is not just about money—it's about gaining control over your life and pursuing your dreams. So, join us on this transformative journey and unleash the power of frugality to unlock a life of financial abundance.

Chapter Two

Goal Setting and Money Mindset

Goal Setting and Money Mindset

G oal Setting and our Money Mindset Overview

Get ready to crush your financial goals with the 30-Day Frugal Living Challenge! This incredible journey towards financial independence and abundance is all about setting goals and taking control of your finances. Are you ready to develop smart spending habits and achieve your wildest financial dreams? Let's dive into this subchapter and discover the power of setting goals for the challenge, and how to do it effectively.

Why Set Goals?

Goals are the driving force behind your success. They give you direction, motivation, and prevent you from getting overwhelmed by the daily demands of life. By setting specific goals for the 30-Day

Frugal Living Challenge, you'll not only stay on track but also measure your progress and celebrate those fantastic victories along the way.

Identifying Your Financial Objectives

Before we embark on this challenge, take some time to identify your financial objectives. Do you want to crush debt, save up for a down payment, or build that emergency fund? Or maybe your goal is early retirement and achieving financial independence (FIRE) whether that be fat FIRE, lean FIRE or barista FIRE . Whatever your dreams may be, grab a pen and write them down, prioritizing them based on their importance to you.

Now, let's make your goals super attainable by following the SMART goal setting framework. SMART stands for Specific, Measurable, Achievable, Relevant, and Time-bound. Instead of setting a vague goal like "save money," let's get specific: "Let's save $500 in the next 30 days by cutting back on dining out and entertainment expenses." Boom! This goal is measurable, achievable within the given time frame, relevant to your financial objectives, and has a clear deadline.

Breaking Down Your Goals

You've set those fantastic financial goals for the 30-Day Frugal Living Challenge, and now it's time to break them down into smaller, actionable steps. If your goal is to save $500, let's determine how much you need to save each week or even each day. Breaking goals down into bite-sized tasks makes them more manageable and keeps you motivated as you see progress being made.

Tracking Your Progress

Now, throughout this fantastic 30-Day Frugal Living Challenge, you need to track your progress regularly. Grab a journal or use a spreadsheet to record your daily expenses, savings, and any challenges you face. This not only keeps you accountable but also empowers you to analyze your spending patterns and make adjustments as needed.

Remember, setting goals for the 30-Day Frugal Living Challenge is just the beginning! Stay committed, embrace the frugal lifestyle, and be ready to rock your way towards financial independence and a life full of abundance. Get excited, because by the end of this challenge, you'll be well on your way to achieving your wildest dreams!Chapter 2: Creating a Frugal Mindset

Examining Your Beliefs and Attitudes Towards Money

Our beliefs and attitudes towards money play a crucial role in shaping our financial situation. They influence the decisions we make, the way we handle money, and ultimately, our ability to achieve financial independence and a life of abundance.

Understanding our beliefs and attitudes towards money is the first step towards creating lasting change in our financial lives. Many of these beliefs are formed early on in our childhood and are influenced by our family, society, and culture. As we grow older, these beliefs become deeply ingrained in our subconscious, guiding our financial choices without us even realizing it.

The 30-day frugal living challenge encourages us to question and examine these beliefs. Are we constantly chasing after material possessions to find happiness? Do we believe that money is scarce and hard to come by? Are we prone to overspending or hoarding money out of fear?

By bringing these beliefs to light, we can start to challenge and reshape them. We can replace limiting beliefs with empowering ones that align with our financial goals. For instance, instead of believing that money is scarce, we can adopt an abundance mindset and believe that there are limitless opportunities to create wealth.

Our attitudes towards money also play a significant role in our financial well-being. Our attitudes determine how we view saving, spending, and investing. Do we see saving as a sacrifice or an investment in our future? Do we view spending as a means to impress others or as a way to enhance our lives? Do we approach investing with fear or as an opportunity for growth?

By examining our attitudes towards money, we can identify any negative patterns that may be holding us back. We can then work towards adopting healthier attitudes that support our financial goals and aspirations.

Ultimately, understanding and examining our beliefs and attitudes towards money is a transformative process. It allows us to take control of our financial destiny and make conscious choices that lead to financial independence and a life of abundance. Through a 30-day frugal living challenge, we can embark on a journey of self-discovery and personal growth, gaining the tools and knowledge to build a solid foundation for our financial future.

Identifying and Overcoming Limiting Financial Mindsets

In our journey towards financial independence and a life of abundance, it is crucial to address the limiting financial mindsets that may be holding us back. These mindsets can prevent us from reaching our full potential and hinder our progress towards our goals. In this subchapter, we will explore common limiting financial mindsets and provide strategies to overcome them.

One of the most common limiting financial mindsets is the belief that we are destined to live paycheck to paycheck and that wealth is only for the lucky few. This mindset can stem from a lack of financial education or negative experiences with money in the past. However, it is essential to understand that wealth creation is within our reach, regardless of our starting point. By shifting our mindset and embracing a growth mentality, we can start taking the necessary steps towards financial independence.

Another limiting mindset is the fear of scarcity and the inability to let go of material possessions. This mindset often leads to excessive spending, accumulating debt, and an inability to save for the future. Overcoming this mindset requires a shift in perspective, recognizing that true abundance comes from experiences, relationships, and personal growth rather than material possessions. Embracing frugality and minimalism can help us break free from this mindset and focus on what truly matters.

Furthermore, the mindset of instant gratification is a significant obstacle to achieving financial independence. In today's consumer-driven society, it is easy to fall into the trap of impulse buying and prioritizing short-term pleasures over long-term financial goals. Overcoming this mindset requires discipline, self-control, and a focus on delayed gratification. By setting clear financial goals and practicing conscious spending, we can gradually shift our mindset towards long-term financial success.

Finally, the mindset of relying solely on a single source of income can be limiting. Many individuals believe that a traditional 9-5 job is the only way to generate income, which can restrict their potential for financial growth. Overcoming this mindset involves exploring alternative income streams such as side hustles, freelancing, or passive income investments. Diversifying our income sources not only provides financial security but also opens up opportunities for personal and professional growth.

By identifying and overcoming these limiting financial mindsets, we can unlock our full potential and embark on a path towards financial independence and a life of abundance. It is essential to recognize that our mindset plays a significant role in our financial journey and that with the right mindset, anything is possible. Embrace the challenge of transforming your financial mindset, and you will be amazed at the opportunities that await you on the path to financial freedom.

Cultivating a Positive Relationship with Money

It's often easy to become overwhelmed and stressed about our finances. However, in order to achieve financial independence and live a life of abundance, it's essential to cultivate a positive relationship with money. This book will guide you through the process of transforming your mindset and developing healthy habits surrounding your finances.

First and foremost, it's important to understand that money is simply a tool. It should not define your self-worth or happiness. By detaching your emotions from money and viewing it as a means to achieve your goals and dreams, you can begin to foster a healthier perspective.

One of the key principles to cultivating a positive relationship with money is practicing gratitude. Take a moment each day to reflect on the financial blessings you have, whether it's a steady income, a roof over your head, or the ability to provide for your loved ones. By acknowledging and appreciating what you already have, you invite more abundance into your life.

Another crucial aspect of developing a healthy relationship with money is practicing mindful spending. Engage in a 30-day frugal living challenge, where you evaluate your expenses and identify areas where you can cut back. This exercise will not only help you save money, but it will also encourage intentional spending and discourage impulsive purchases.

To further enhance your financial well-being, it's important to set clear financial goals. Whether it's saving for retirement, paying off debt, or purchasing a home, having a vision for your financial future provides motivation and direction. Break down these goals into smaller, achievable milestones, and celebrate each success along the way.

In addition to setting goals, it's crucial to develop a budget and stick to it. Track your income and expenses meticulously, and allocate a certain percentage towards savings and investments. This will help you stay on track and make informed decisions about your financial priorities.

Finally, surround yourself with like-minded individuals who share your interest in personal finance and frugal living. Join online communities, attend local meetups, or find a financial mentor who can provide guidance and support. Surrounding yourself with a positive and supportive network will not only inspire you, but also hold you accountable on your journey towards financial independence.

Remember, cultivating a positive relationship with money is a life-long journey. By embracing gratitude, practicing mindful spending, setting goals, and seeking support, you can transform your financial mindset and unlock a life of abundance and freedom.

Chapter Three

Assessing Your Current Financial Situation

Assessing Your Current Financial Situation

Tracking Your Income and Expenses

I n the journey towards financial independence and a life of abundance, one essential tool you need in your arsenal is the ability to track your income and expenses effectively. The process of monitoring your financial inflows and outflows, helps you gain better control over your money and make more informed decisions.

Why is tracking your income and expenses important? Simply put, it provides you with a clear picture of where your money is coming from and where it is going. By understanding your income sources and expenditure patterns, you can identify areas where you can cut back, save more, and invest wisely.

To begin tracking your income, start by documenting all sources of revenue, including your salary, side hustles, rental income, and any other monetary inflows. This will give you a comprehensive overview of your total income and enable you to set realistic financial goals. Additionally, tracking your income allows you to identify potential opportunities to increase your earnings, such as negotiating a raise or exploring new income streams.

Next, it's time to delve into tracking your expenses. Create a detailed list of all your monthly expenses, including fixed costs like rent, utilities, and loan repayments, as well as variable expenses like groceries, transportation, and entertainment. Categorize your expenses to gain a better understanding of where your money is going and identify areas where you can cut back or optimize spending.

There are various methods you can use to track your income and expenses effectively. Traditional methods include using spreadsheets or notebooks, while technological advancements have introduced user-friendly budgeting apps and online tools that automate the process for you. Choose a method that suits your preferences and lifestyle, ensuring you can easily update and review your financial records regularly. Personally I like to see it all written down on paper and will do this monthly. I tried a spreadsheet but this doesn't work as well for me. there is no right or wrong method of recording.

Regularly reviewing your income and expenses will allow you to identify any financial leaks and make adjustments accordingly. Analyze your spending habits and assess whether your expenditures align with your financial goals. This knowledge will empower you to make conscious choices about your spending and prioritize investments that will help you achieve financial independence.

By diligently monitoring your financial inflows and outflows, you gain control over your money and can make informed decisions about your spending and saving habits. Start tracking today and take charge of your financial future!

Analyzing Your Spending Patterns

Understanding your spending patterns is a crucial step in achieving financial independence and living a life of abundance. Analyzing your expenses helps you in identifying areas where you can cut back, and ultimately, adopting a frugal lifestyle that aligns with your financial goals.

To begin, it's essential to track your spending for a certain period, preferably a month. This exercise will provide you with a comprehensive overview of where your money is going. Use a budgeting app or simply create a spreadsheet to record each expense, categorizing them into essential and non-essential categories. By doing this, you will gain clarity about your spending habits and uncover areas where you can make significant changes.

Once you have a clear picture of your spending, it's time to evaluate each expense critically. Start by identifying your non-essential expenses, such as dining out, entertainment, or impulse purchases. These are often the areas where we unconsciously spend a significant portion of our income. By scrutinizing these expenses, you can begin to find alternative, more frugal options that will help you save money without sacrificing enjoyment.

Next, focus on your essential expenses, such as rent or mortgage, utilities, and groceries. Look for ways to reduce costs without compromising your quality of life. For example, you could consider downsizing your living space, negotiating better deals with service providers, or adopting a more economical approach to grocery shopping.

As you analyze your spending patterns, it's crucial to differentiate between needs and wants. By distinguishing between the two, you can prioritize your spending on essential items and allocate any extra funds towards your financial goals, such as paying off debt or building an emergency fund.

Additionally, take the time to reflect on your emotional triggers for spending. Are you prone to impulse purchases when feeling stressed or unhappy? Understanding your emotional relationship with money will help you make more conscious decisions and avoid falling into unnecessary spending patterns.

By analyzing your spending patterns and implementing strategic changes, you will gradually develop a frugal mindset that supports your journey towards financial independence. Remember, frugality does not mean deprivation; it means making intentional choices that align with your values and long-term goals.

Identifying Areas of Overspending and Waste

In our quest for financial independence and a life of abundance, it is crucial to take a closer look at our spending habits and identify areas where we may be overspending or wasting money. By doing so, we can make informed decisions and take necessary steps towards a more frugal lifestyle, ultimately achieving our financial goals.

After we track our expenses diligently and analyze our spending we can look at areas of waste or spend not in line with our bigger life of abundance picture. This involves keeping a record of every single purchase we make, whether it's a cup of coffee or a major household expense. By analyzing our expenditure patterns, we can quickly spot areas where our spending exceeds our budget or where our money is being wasted.

One common area of overspending is dining out at restaurants. While it's enjoyable to treat ourselves occasionally, frequent visits to restaurants can add up quickly and eat into our budget. By cooking meals at home and planning our weekly menus, we can save a significant amount of money and still enjoy delicious and healthy meals.

Another area where overspending often occurs is in our entertainment budget. Subscriptions to multiple streaming services, cable packages, and impulse purchases of books or movies can all contribute to unnecessary expenses. By reviewing our entertainment choices and opting for more cost-effective alternatives, such as libraries or free online resources, we can save a substantial amount of money without compromising on our leisure activities.

Additionally, it is essential to scrutinize our utility bills and find ways to reduce energy consumption. Simple steps like turning off lights when leaving a room, unplugging electronic devices when not in use, and properly insulating our homes can result in significant savings on our monthly bills.

Identifying areas of overspending and waste also requires us to examine our shopping habits. Impulsive purchases, buying items we don't need, and falling prey to sales and marketing tactics can drain our finances. By adopting a more mindful approach to shopping, creating a list before heading to the store, and practicing delayed gratification, we can avoid unnecessary purchases and save money for more meaningful experiences.

Identifying areas of overspending and waste is a crucial step towards achieving financial independence and living a life of abundance. By diligently tracking our expenses, analyzing our spending patterns, and making conscious choices, we can identify and eliminate wasteful habits. This preparation part of a 30 day frugal challenge helps readers interested in personal finance, self-development, and frugal living to take control of their finances, embark on a life changing 30-day frugal living challenge, and pave the way towards a financially secure future.

Chapter Four

Creating a Budget and Savings Plan

Creating a Budget and Savings Plan

Developing a Realistic Budget

C reating a budget is an essential step towards achieving financial independence and living a life of abundance. It allows you to take control of your finances, prioritize your spending, and work towards your goals. In this section, we will explore the process of developing a realistic budget that aligns with your values and supports your journey towards financial independence.

Step 1: Assess Your Current Financial Situation
Before diving into budgeting, it's crucial to have a clear understanding

of your current financial situation. Take a comprehensive look at your income, expenses, debts, and savings. This will help you identify areas where you can cut back and areas where you can allocate more funds.

Step 2: Set Clear Financial Goals

Define your financial goals and aspirations. Whether you are saving for retirement, paying off debt, or planning for a vacation, having specific targets will guide your budgeting decisions. Set short-term and long-term goals to keep yourself motivated throughout the process.

Step 3: Track Your Expenses

Tracking your expenses is essential to identify spending patterns and areas where you can make adjustments. Take note of every dollar you spend for at least a month, categorizing expenses into fixed (rent, utilities) and variable (entertainment, dining out). This will give you a holistic view of your spending habits.

Step 4: Prioritize Your Spending

Once you have a clear understanding of your expenses, it's time to prioritize. Differentiate between needs and wants, and allocate your funds accordingly. Focus on essentials like housing, food, and healthcare first, and then allocate remaining funds towards your financial goals.

Step 5: Cut Back on Unnecessary Expenses

Identify areas where you can cut back and reduce unnecessary expenses. This could involve cooking at home more often, canceling unused subscriptions, or finding cheaper alternatives for your daily needs. Every dollar saved can be redirected towards your financial goals.

Step 6: Review and Adjust Regularly

Budgeting is an ongoing process. It's important to review your budget regularly, ideally on a monthly basis, to ensure it remains realistic and adaptable to your changing circumstances. Life happens, and your budget should be flexible enough to accommodate unexpected expenses or changes in income.

By following these steps and developing a realistic budget, you are taking a crucial step towards financial independence and a life of abundance. Remember, frugality is not about deprivation but about making conscious choices that align with your values and goals. Start your 30-day frugal living challenge today and witness the positive impact it can have on your personal finance journey.

Strategies for Cutting Expenses

It's easy to fall into the trap of overspending and living beyond our means. However, by adopting a frugal lifestyle and implementing strategies to cut expenses, we can take control of our finances and pave the way for financial independence and a life of abundance. Some effective strategies that will help you embrace frugality and make significant progress towards your financial goals include the following:

1. Create a Budget: As outlined, it is important to have a clear understanding of your income and expenses. Create a monthly budget and track your spending meticulously. Identify areas where you can reduce costs and set realistic goals to achieve financial stability.

2. Eliminate Debt: High-interest debt can quickly drain your finances. Develop a plan to pay off your debts, starting with the ones with the highest interest rates. Consider consolidating your debts or negotiating lower interest rates with your creditors.

3. Embrace Minimalism: Adopting a minimalist lifestyle can be liberating and help you cut unnecessary expenses. Declutter your living space and prioritize experiences over material possessions. Before making a purchase, ask yourself if it aligns with your values and if you truly need it.

4. Shop Smart: Make it a habit to compare prices, look for deals, and use coupons when shopping for groceries or other necessities. Consider buying in bulk or purchasing generic brands to save money. Plan your meals in advance and cook at home, rather than eating out frequently.

5. Reduce Utility Bills: Take simple steps to reduce your utility bills. Turn off lights and appliances when not in use, unplug electronics, and use energy-efficient bulbs. Lower your thermostat in winter and use fans instead of air conditioning in summer. Insulate your home and seal any drafts to reduce heating and cooling costs.

6. Cut Subscription Services: Evaluate your monthly subscriptions and determine if they are truly worth the cost. Cancel unnecessary subscriptions like cable TV, streaming services, or gym memberships that you rarely use. Look for free or low-cost alternatives for entertainment and exercise.

7. Emphasize DIY: Develop new skills and take on do-it-yourself projects to save money. Learn to cook, mend clothes, or fix minor household repairs instead of hiring professionals. Embrace the satisfaction and cost-saving benefits of doing things yourself.

By implementing these strategies and committing to a frugal lifestyle, you can take control of your finances and work towards financial independence. Remember, it's not about depriving yourself of necessities or enjoyment, but rather making intentional choices that align with your goals and values. A 30-day frugal living challenge done once or twice a year to a stricter set of rules you set for yourself will reset your mindset and transform your financial future.

Setting Up an Emergency Fund

In the journey towards financial independence and a life of abundance, one crucial step is to set up an emergency fund. Life is unpredictable, and unexpected expenses can arise at any moment. Whether it's a medical emergency, a car repair, or a sudden job loss, having a safety net in the form of an emergency fund can provide peace of mind and financial security.

So, what exactly is an emergency fund? It's a pool of money set aside specifically for unforeseen circumstances. This fund should be easily accessible, preferably in a separate savings account, and should only be used for true emergencies. It is not to be confused with a regular savings account or a vacation fund.

To start building your emergency fund, you need to determine how much you should save. A general rule of thumb is to aim for at least three to six months' worth of living expenses. Consider your monthly bills, groceries, rent or mortgage, and other essential expenses. Calculate the total and set a realistic goal for your emergency fund.

The next step is to automate your savings. Treat your emergency fund as a non-negotiable expense. Set up automatic transfers from your checking account to your emergency fund every payday. By automating this process, you'll ensure consistent contributions towards your fund without the temptation to spend that money elsewhere.

When it comes to choosing the right account for your emergency fund, look for one that offers a high-yield savings account with minimal fees. This will help your money grow over time and keep it separate from your day-to-day spending.

Remember, emergencies can happen at any time, so it's essential to prioritize building your emergency fund. Cut back on unnecessary expenses, find ways to increase your income, and redirect those savings towards your fund. Consider adopting a frugal lifestyle, where you consciously choose to spend less on non-essential items.

Building an emergency fund is not a one-time task; it requires on-going commitment and regular contributions. As you work towards your goal, celebrate small milestones along the way. Every dollar saved brings you one step closer to financial security and that feeling abundance that is the goal of 30 day spending challenges.

An emergency fund is a critical component of achieving financial independence. By establishing this safety net, you'll be better prepared to handle unexpected expenses without derailing your progress. Start today, and make it a priority to build your emergency fund. Your future self will thank you for it.

Chapter Five

Frugal Meal Planning and Grocery Shopping

Frugal Meal Planning and Grocery Shopping

Planning Meals on a Budget

T oday, where expenses seem to be constantly on the rise, it's essential to find ways to save money without compromising on our health and well-being. One area where we can significantly cut down our expenses is our grocery bills, specifically by planning meals on a budget. Below we outline some practical strategies and tips to help you eat delicious and nutritious meals while keeping your wallet happy.

1. Assess Your Pantry: Before planning any meals, take inventory of your pantry and fridge. Identify the ingredients you already have and can use in upcoming meals. This step will help you reduce waste and save money by utilizing what you already have on hand.

2. Plan Weekly Menus: Creating a weekly menu not only saves you time but also helps you stay organized and stick to your budget. Start by listing the meals you want to prepare for the upcoming week, considering your family's preferences and dietary needs. Look for recipes that use similar ingredients to minimize waste and save money.

3. Shop with a Grocery List: Never go grocery shopping without a well-thought-out list. With a list in hand, you'll be less likely to buy unnecessary items or impulse purchases. Stick to your list, purchasing only the items you need for your planned meals.

4. Embrace Seasonal and Sale Items: Opt for seasonal produce and sale items, as they are typically more affordable and fresher. Plan your meals around these ingredients to take advantage of their lower prices while adding variety to your diet.

5. Cook in Batches: Prepare meals in bulk and freeze them in individual portions. This strategy not only saves you money but also saves time on busy days. Batch cooking allows you to take advantage of bulk discounts, reduces food waste, and ensures you always have a home-cooked meal ready to go.

6. Use Coupons and Discounts: Keep an eye out for coupons and discounts on your favorite grocery items. Websites, apps, and local flyers often offer great deals that can help you save money while planning your meals.

7. DIY and Avoid Processed Foods: Opting for homemade meals instead of heavily processed, pre-packaged foods is a healthier and

more cost-effective choice. Cooking from scratch allows you to control the ingredients and flavors while saving money in the long run.

Remember, planning meals on a budget is not about sacrificing taste or nutrition. It's about being mindful of your spending while still enjoying delicious, affordable, and healthy meals. By implementing these strategies, you'll not only save money but also develop good financial habits and a frugal mindset that will benefit you in the long run.

Strategies for Smart Grocery Shopping

All around the post-Covid world, expenses seem to be constantly on the rise, so it's important to find ways to save money wherever possible. One area where you can make a significant impact on your monthly budget is through smart grocery shopping. By adopting some proven strategies, you can save money, reduce waste, and still eat well. In this section, we will explore several strategies for smart grocery shopping that will help you on your frugal living journey.

1. Make a List and Stick to It: As outlined earlier, before heading to the grocery store, take some time to plan your meals for the week. Create a detailed list of the items you need, and stick to it. This will prevent impulse purchases and ensure you only buy what you actually need.

2. Shop with a Full Stomach: Shopping on an empty stomach can lead to unnecessary purchases, as hunger can cloud your judgment. Always eat before heading to the grocery store to avoid falling into this trap.

3. Compare Prices: Don't settle for the first product you see. Take the time to compare prices and find the best deals. Consider switching to cheaper brands or trying store brands, as they are often just as

good as their more expensive counterparts. Also check out different supermarkets for cheaper options

4. Shop in Bulk: Buying in bulk can save you a significant amount of money in the long run. Look for deals on non-perishable items or items that you use frequently. Just make sure you have enough storage space to accommodate your purchases.

5. Use Coupons and Cashback Apps: Take advantage of coupons and cashback apps to maximize your savings. Many grocery stores offer digital coupons that can be easily added to your loyalty card. Additionally, cashback apps allow you to earn money back on your purchases.

6. Avoid Shopping When You're in a Rush: When you're in a hurry, you're more likely to make impulsive decisions and overspend. Set aside dedicated time for grocery shopping to ensure you can take your time and make wise choices.

7. Buy Seasonal and Local Produce: Seasonal and local produce tends to be cheaper and fresher than imported options. Take advantage of what's in season and support local farmers while saving money.

By implementing these strategies you can make a significant impact on your monthly budget. Start incorporating these strategies into your routine and enjoy the benefits of both financial independence and a life of abundance.

Cooking and Meal Prepping for Savings

In our quest for financial independence and a life of abundance, one area that often gets overlooked is our food expenses. It's no secret that eating out can quickly drain our wallets, but did you know that cooking and meal prepping at home can save you a significant amount of money? There are so many health and financial benefits of cooking and meal prepping. Its good to explore practical tips for incorporating this frugal habit into your daily life and develop some strategies that fit within your life.

When it comes to personal finance, food is one of the most flexible areas where we can cut costs. By cooking at home, you have complete control over your ingredients, portion sizes, and cooking methods. Not only does this give you the opportunity to make healthier choices, but it also allows you to save a substantial amount of money. Eating out can easily cost two to three times more than preparing a meal at home, especially if you're dining at restaurants frequently.

Meal prepping is another powerful tool in your frugal living arsenal. By dedicating a few hours each week to plan and prepare your meals in advance, you can save both time and money. Imagine coming home after a long day and having a delicious, homemade meal ready to enjoy within minutes! Meal prepping not only eliminates the need for expensive takeout or delivery, but it also reduces food waste and helps you stick to your budget.

Review and research meal planning templates, budget-friendly recipes, and time-saving tips to help you get started; Amazon, Youtube and general google searches will help you find meals that appeal to you with preparation that suits your lifestyle. Learn how to create a well-balanced meal plan, shop smartly for groceries, and make the most out of your ingredients. Explore Air Fryer and Crockpot meals, meals that are good to freeze or easy bake dishes that are nutritious and also healthy to the body and the hip pocket.

Over your 30 day challenge you will have gained the knowledge and confidence to embrace cooking and meal prepping as powerful tools for saving money, improving your health, and achieving financial independence.

Remember, financial independence is not about sacrificing the things you love; it's about making intentional choices that align with your long-term goals. Cooking and meal prepping for savings is not only a practical and frugal habit but also a rewarding and enjoyable experience that will bring you one step closer to a life of abundance.

Chapter Six

Minimizing Your Possessions and Decluttering

Minimizing Your Possessions and Decluttering

Understanding the Benefits of Minimalism

The concept of minimalism has gained significant traction since Marie Kondo asked us what sparked our joy. Minimalism is not just about decluttering your physical space; it's a mindset that can positively impact every aspect of your life. In this chapter, we will explore the numerous benefits of embracing minimalism and how it can lead to financial independence and a life of abundance.

One of the primary advantages of minimalism is its direct impact on personal finance. By adopting a minimalist lifestyle, you prioritize your spending and focus on what truly matters. This means cutting out unnecessary expenses and avoiding the trap of mindless consumerism. As a result, you save money and have more resources to invest in your future. The 30-day frugal living challenge outlined in this book will guide you through actionable steps to achieve financial freedom through minimalism.

Furthermore, minimalism helps you develop a stronger sense of self and purpose. By letting go of material possessions and external validation, you gain clarity about what truly brings you joy and fulfillment. This self-awareness allows you to make intentional choices in all areas of your life, from career decisions to relationships. With minimalism, you begin to focus on experiences, relationships, and personal growth, leading to a more meaningful and abundant life.

Another benefit of minimalism is the reduction of stress and overwhelm. In today's society, we are bombarded with information, distractions, and an endless stream of possessions. By decluttering your physical space and simplifying your life, you create a peaceful environment that promotes calmness and clarity. This, in turn, boosts your overall well-being and mental health.

Minimalism also contributes to environmental sustainability. By reducing consumption and waste, you actively participate in the preservation of our planet. The minimalist lifestyle promotes conscious choices, such as buying second-hand, repurposing items, and reducing energy consumption. These small changes collectively make a significant impact on the environment and contribute to a greener future.

Understanding and embracing the benefits of minimalism can truly transform your life. By focusing on what truly matters, you can achieve financial independence, experience personal growth, reduce stress, and contribute to a sustainable world. The 30-day frugal living challenge presented in this book will help provide you with practical tools and strategies to integrate minimalism into your daily life. Putting them into practice over your own 30 day challenge will truly change your life and direct you to a life of freedom and abundance.

Decluttering Your Home and Spaces

Simply put, It's easy to accumulate stuff. Our homes become filled with items we no longer use or need, and our spaces become cluttered and chaotic. But did you know that decluttering your home can have a profound impact not only on your physical space but also on your mental and financial well-being?

Decluttering has benefits in achieving financial independence and living a life of abundance. Whether you're a minimalist at heart or simply looking to streamline your life, this 30-day frugal living challenge will help you transform your living spaces and, ultimately, your mindset.

By letting go of excess possessions, you'll find yourself spending less on unnecessary purchases and becoming more mindful of your spending habits. Decluttering can also help you uncover hidden treasures that you can sell or repurpose, adding an extra income stream to your journey towards financial independence. There are many ideas and methods of decluttering but choose one that works for you.

The Marie Kondo method is a popular organization and decluttering approach. It focuses on keeping items that spark joy and discarding those that do not. The method involves categories like clothing, books, and sentimental items. It emphasizes tidying by category rather than location. The KonMari method also advocates for proper storage and organization of belongings. Overall, it aims to create a more harmonious and joyful living space.

The 80 20 rule of decluttering, also known as the Pareto Principle, suggests that we use 20% of our belongings 80% of the time. This rule can be applied to decluttering our homes by focusing on the 20% of our possessions that we use most frequently and getting rid of the rest. By identifying and keeping the most essential items, we can reduce clutter and create a more organized living space. This principle can also be applied to other areas of life, such as time management and productivity, by focusing on the most important tasks and activities that yield the greatest results.

But decluttering isn't just about physical possessions. We'll also explore how to declutter your digital life, including your email inbox, social media accounts, and digital files. By eliminating digital clutter, you'll free up mental space and increase your productivity, ultimately helping you achieve your financial goals faster.

Throughout your own30-day frugal living challenge, you'll discover the joy of living with less, the satisfaction of an organized space, and the financial freedom that comes from embracing frugality.

Selling, Donating, or Repurposing Unwanted Items

One of the key principles of frugal living is to make the most of what you already have. This includes finding new purposes for items you no longer need or want.

When it comes to selling unwanted items, there are numerous platforms available to help you reach potential buyers. Online marketplaces such as eBay, Craigslist, and Facebook Marketplace allow you to list items and connect with interested buyers in your local area. Take some time to research the best platform for your specific item and price it accordingly. Remember, one person's trash could be another person's treasure!

If the thought of selling seems too time-consuming or daunting, donating is a wonderful alternative. Many charities and organizations accept donations of gently used items, such as clothing, furniture, and household goods. Donating not only helps declutter your space but also supports those in need. Research local charities in your area and find out what items they accept. You may even be eligible for a tax deduction, so be sure to keep track of your donations.

Repurposing unwanted items is another creative way to extend their lifespan and reduce waste. Get crafty and think outside the box! For example, an old wooden ladder can be transformed into a unique bookshelf, or mason jars can become stylish storage containers. Pinterest and other DIY websites offer endless inspiration for repurposing ideas. Not only will you save money by repurposing, but you'll also add a touch of personal style to your home.

To make the most of this frugal living challenge, set aside some time each week to assess your belongings and determine what can be sold, donated, or repurposed. Create a designated area in your home to organize these items, making it easier to keep track of what needs to go where. Remember, the goal is not just to declutter but also to maximize the value of your unwanted items.

Chapter Seven

Frugal Entertainment and Leisure

Frugal Entertainment and Leisure

Discovering Free or Low-Cost Activities

It's easy to get caught up in the idea that spending money equals having a good time. But what if I told you that you could have just as much fun, if not more, by engaging in free or low-cost activities? In this section we will explore the world of frugal entertainment and discover the abundance of joy that can be found without breaking the bank.

1. Embrace the Great Outdoors: Nature has a way of providing endless entertainment at no cost. Take a hike in a nearby park, have

a picnic in your backyard, or go for a swim in a local lake. Not only will you save money, but you'll also reap the benefits of fresh air and exercise.

2. Dive into the World of Books: Libraries are a treasure trove of free entertainment. Dive into a captivating novel, learn a new skill from a how-to book, or explore the latest bestsellers. You'll be amazed at the wealth of knowledge and entertainment waiting for you on those library shelves.

3. Unleash Your Creativity: Engage in artistic endeavors such as painting, drawing, or writing. These activities not only provide a sense of fulfillment but also offer an opportunity for self-expression and personal growth. You don't need expensive supplies to get started; a simple pen and paper can unlock a whole new world of creativity.

4. Explore Local Events: Keep an eye out for free or low-cost events happening in your community. From concerts in the park to art exhibits, there is always something happening that won't cost you a fortune. Check community bulletin boards, local newspapers, and social media platforms for updates on upcoming events.

5. Volunteer: Giving back to your community is not only a rewarding experience but also a great way to engage in free activities. Volunteer at a local charity, help organize a community event, or offer your skills to those in need. Not only will you make a difference in the lives of others, but you'll also meet new people and gain valuable experiences.

Remember, the key to frugal living is not deprivation but rather finding joy in the simple things. By embracing free or low-cost activities, you can lead a life of abundance without straining your finances. So go ahead, discover the wealth of entertainment that awaits you without spending a dime.

DIY Hobbies and Creative Pursuits

In our busy work and chore focused life, finding meaningful and fulfilling hobbies can be a challenge. We often find ourselves spending our free time mindlessly scrolling through social media or binge-watching the latest TV series. However, there is a vast array of DIY hobbies and creative pursuits that not only provide entertainment but also contribute to our personal development and financial independence.

Why DIY Hobbies?

Engaging in DIY hobbies and creative pursuits is not just about saving money; it's about embracing a frugal mindset and cultivating a life of abundance. By taking the time to learn new skills and create things with our own hands, we tap into our innate creativity and resourcefulness. DIY hobbies allow us to express ourselves, reduce stress, and develop a sense of accomplishment.

Exploring Various DIY Hobbies

From woodworking and gardening to cooking and knitting, there are countless DIY hobbies to choose from. In this section, we will delve into some popular options and provide step-by-step guides to get you started. Learn how to create your own upcycled furniture pieces, grow your own organic vegetables, master the art of homemade bread, or knit cozy scarves and blankets for your loved ones. We will also discuss the benefits of these hobbies, such as cost savings, self-sufficiency, and the joy of creating something unique.

Financial Independence and DIY Hobbies

One of the key aspects of achieving financial independence is reducing unnecessary expenses. As you embark on the 30-day frugal living challenge, incorporating DIY hobbies into your daily routine can significantly contribute to your financial goals. Instead of buying expensive home decor, you can create your own personalized pieces. Rather than dining out, you can prepare delicious meals using ingredients from your garden. By embracing the DIY mindset, you not only save money but also develop valuable skills that can lead to additional income streams.

Embracing a Life of Abundance

DIY hobbies and creative pursuits not only enhance your financial well-being but also contribute to a life of abundance. By engaging in these activities, you tap into your creativity, foster a sense of accomplishment, and connect with like-minded individuals. DIY hobbies provide an avenue for personal growth and self-development, allowing you to discover hidden talents and find joy in the process of creation.

Whether you're a seasoned DIY enthusiast or a beginner looking to explore new hobbies, get ready to unleash your creativity and embark on an exciting journey towards a frugal, fulfilling, and abundant life.

Finding Affordable Ways to Relax and Unwind

In addition to hobbies, finding time to relax and unwind is essential for our overall well-being. However, many people believe that relaxation comes with a hefty price tag. Here, we will explore various affordable ways to find peace and tranquility without breaking the bank.

1. Embrace Nature: One of the simplest and most budget-friendly ways to relax is by immersing yourself in nature. Take a leisurely walk in a nearby park, hike a local trail, or simply sit in your backyard and enjoy the beauty of nature. Connecting with the outdoors can be incredibly soothing and rejuvenating.

2. Practice Meditation and Mindfulness: Meditation and mindfulness are powerful tools that can help you relax and reduce stress. There

are numerous free resources available online, such as guided meditation apps and YouTube videos, that can assist you in developing a regular meditation practice without spending a dime.

3. Create a Self-Care Routine: Self-care doesn't have to be expensive. Dedicate some time each day to activities that bring you joy and relaxation. This could include taking a warm bath, reading a book, practicing yoga, or listening to calming music. By prioritizing self-care, you will find yourself feeling more refreshed and rejuvenated.

4. Explore Free or Low-Cost Hobbies: Engaging in hobbies is a great way to unwind and find joy. Look for activities that interest you and are within your budget. For instance, you could try painting, writing, gardening, or even learning a new instrument. The possibilities are endless, and many hobbies can be pursued at little to no cost as outline din above section

5. Utilize Public Resources: Many communities offer free or low-cost resources for relaxation. Visit your local library and borrow books, audiobooks, or movies to enjoy in your leisure time. Additionally, public parks often organize free yoga or meditation classes. Take advantage of these opportunities to relax without spending a fortune.

Remember, relaxation and self-care are crucial aspects of leading a fulfilled life. By finding affordable ways to unwind, you can prioritize your well-being without compromising your financial goals. Incorporate these tips into your daily routine, and you'll soon discover that relaxation doesn't have to come with a hefty price tag.

Chapter Eight

Saving on Utilities and Household Expenses

Saving on Utilities and Household Expenses

Energy-Saving Tips for Your Home

E nergy costs are constantly on the rise, so finding ways to reduce your monthly expenses without compromising your lifestyle is a top priority. One area where you can make a significant impact is by implementing energy-saving practices in your home. Not only will this help you save money, but it will also contribute to a more sustainable future. In this subchapter, we will explore some practical tips and tricks to help you cut down on energy consumption and lower your utility bills.

1. Upgrade to energy-efficient appliances: Consider replacing old, energy-guzzling appliances with energy-efficient models. Look for the ENERGY STAR label when purchasing new refrigerators, dishwashers, washing machines, and air conditioners. These appliances are designed to use less electricity while maintaining optimal performance.

2. Insulate your home: Proper insulation is key to keeping your home comfortable and energy-efficient. Insulate your walls, attic, and crawl spaces to prevent heat loss during winter and keep cool air inside during summer. Install weatherstripping around doors and windows to seal any air leaks.

3. Optimize your heating and cooling systems: Set your thermostat to an energy-saving temperature, such as 68°F (20°C) during winter and 78°F (25°C) during summer. Use programmable thermostats to automatically adjust the temperature when you're away from home. Regularly clean or replace air filters to ensure optimal airflow.

4. Utilize natural lighting: Take advantage of natural light by opening curtains and blinds during the day. This not only reduces the need for artificial lighting but also helps heat your home during winter. Install skylights or solar tubes in rooms that lack adequate natural light.

5. Unplug electronics when not in use: Many electronic devices continue to consume energy even when turned off. To prevent this "phantom" energy usage, unplug chargers, televisions, computers, and other electronics when not in use, or use power strips with an on/off switch.

6. Switch to LED light bulbs: LED bulbs are not only more energy-efficient but also last significantly longer than traditional incandescent bulbs. Replace your old light bulbs with LEDs to save on energy costs and reduce the frequency of replacements.

By implementing these energy-saving tips in your home, you will not only reduce your carbon footprint but also enjoy substantial savings on your utility bills. Remember, small changes can make a big difference.

Reducing Water Usage and Waste

Water is a valuable resource that we often take for granted. In our pursuit of financial independence and a life of abundance, it is important to be mindful of our water consumption and make efforts to reduce waste. Not only does this help the environment, but it can also save us money in the long run. In this chapter, we will explore various strategies to minimize water usage and waste during our 30-day frugal living challenge.

One of the simplest ways to reduce water usage is by being mindful of our daily habits. Turning off the tap while brushing our teeth or lathering our hands can save gallons of water each day. Similarly, taking shorter showers and installing low-flow showerheads can significantly reduce water consumption without sacrificing personal hygiene.

Another area where we can make a big impact is in our outdoor water usage. Instead of using sprinklers to water our lawns, consider using a drip irrigation system or watering by hand. This ensures that water is delivered directly to the plant roots, minimizing evaporation and waste. Additionally, collecting rainwater in barrels can provide a free and sustainable source of water for outdoor plants.

In the kitchen, we can make conscious decisions to reduce water waste. For example, instead of running the tap to defrost frozen food, plan ahead and thaw it in the refrigerator overnight. Furthermore, using a dishwasher instead of hand-washing dishes can actually save water, as modern dishwashers are designed to be more efficient. Just make sure to run full loads and skip the pre-rinse step to maximize water savings.

Lastly, we should check our homes for any leaks or drips that may be wasting water unnoticed. A dripping faucet may seem insignificant, but over time, it can waste hundreds of gallons of water. Fixing these leaks not only conserves water but also prevents unnecessary expenses on water bills.

By implementing these strategies, we can significantly reduce our water usage and waste. Not only will this positively impact the environment, but it will also contribute to our financial well-being. Together, we can create a more sustainable future while achieving our goals of financial independence and abundance.

Cutting Costs on Internet, Cable, and Phone Services

In today's digital age, internet, cable, and phone services have become an integral part of our lives. However, the ever-increasing costs associated with these services can put a strain on our finances. Thankfully, there are several ways to cut down on these expenses without sacrificing the quality of your connection or the entertainment options available to you.

One of the first steps towards reducing your costs is to assess your current usage and needs. Do you really need that expensive cable package with hundreds of channels when you only watch a handful? Consider downsizing to a more affordable plan or even cutting the cord altogether and switching to streaming services that offer a wide range of content at a fraction of the cost.

Similarly, take a close look at your internet usage. Are you paying for higher speeds than you actually need? Downgrading to a more basic plan could save you a significant amount each month. Additionally, consider bundling your internet and cable services with a single provider. Many companies offer discounts for bundled services, helping you save even more.

When it comes to phone services, explore alternatives to traditional landlines and cell phone plans. Voice over Internet Protocol (VoIP) services like Skype or Google Voice allow you to make calls over the internet at a much lower cost. Alternatively, consider switching to a cheaper prepaid cell phone plan or exploring options provided by smaller, more affordable carriers.

Another effective strategy for cutting costs is to negotiate with your service providers. Many companies are willing to offer discounts or promotional rates to retain their customers. Give them a call and inquire about any available deals or loyalty programs. It never hurts to ask, and you may be pleasantly surprised by the savings you can achieve.

Finally, keep an eye out for special promotions and deals. Providers often offer introductory rates or limited-time offers that can significantly reduce your monthly expenses. Stay informed by regularly checking websites, signing up for newsletters, or following social media accounts of the service providers you are interested in. By implementing these strategies, you can effectively reduce your internet, cable, and phone expenses, putting more money back into your pocket.

Chapter Nine

Building Multiple Streams of Income

Building Multiple Streams of Income

Exploring Side Hustle Opportunities

It's becoming more and more crucial to discover methods to increase our earnings and attain financial freedom. While saving and reducing costs are essential in reaching our financial objectives, exploring additional income opportunities can significantly impact our path toward prosperity.

A side hustle is a part-time job or business venture that allows individuals to generate additional income outside of their regular jobs. It provides an avenue for exploring our passions, honing our skills, and diversifying our income streams. Whether you're looking to pay off debt, save for retirement, or simply have some extra cash for life's pleasures, side hustles can play a significant role in accelerating your progress.

From freelance writing, graphic design, and virtual assistance to tutoring, pet sitting, and even renting out your spare room on Airbnb, there are countless ways to turn your hobbies and talents into profitable ventures.

The gig economy economy is a growing field and you can explore platforms such as Uber, TaskRabbit, and Upwork that connect individuals with freelance work opportunities. These platforms offer flexibility and freedom to work on your terms, allowing you to earn money on your schedule.

Furthermore, technology can be leveraged to maximize our side hustle potential. With the advent of the internet and social media, the opportunities for remote work and online businesses have expanded exponentially. The world of e-commerce, affiliate marketing, and content creation, shows you how to build a successful online presence and monetize your digital assets.

Additionally, in any frugal challenge it is important to balance your side hustle with your day job and personal life, and set realistic expectations for your financial goals. It's crucial to approach side hustles with a strategic mindset and a clear understanding of your priorities.

Exploring side hustle opportunities can be an exciting and fulfilling journey towards financial independence. By diversifying your income streams and tapping into your passions and skills, you can create a life of abundance while pursuing your financial goals. So, let's embark on this exploration together and unlock the potential within you to achieve financial independence and live a life of frugal abundance.

Investing for Passive Income

The ability to generate passive income has become increasingly important. Whether you're dreaming of early retirement or simply want to create a life of financial abundance, investing for passive income is a key strategy to achieve these goals. This subchapter will provide you with valuable insights and practical tips on how to invest wisely to generate passive income and build long-term wealth.

When it comes to investing for passive income, diversification is crucial. Instead of putting all your eggs in one basket, consider spreading your investments across different asset classes such as stocks, bonds, real estate, and even peer-to-peer lending platforms. This diversification not only helps to mitigate risks but also ensures a steady stream of passive income from various sources.

One popular investment strategy for generating passive income is dividend investing. Dividend stocks are shares of companies that distribute a portion of their profits to shareholders on a regular basis. By investing in dividend-paying stocks, you can earn passive income in the form of regular dividend payments. Additionally, reinvesting these dividends through a dividend reinvestment plan (DRIP) can compound your returns over time, boosting your passive income even further.

Real estate investment trusts (REITs) are another attractive option for passive income seekers. REITs are companies that own and manage income-generating properties, such as apartment complexes, office buildings, and shopping malls. By investing in REITs, you can earn a share of the rental income generated by these properties without the hassle of being a landlord.

If you prefer a more hands-off approach, consider investing in index funds or exchange-traded funds (ETFs). These funds track a specific market index, such as the S&P 500, and offer a diversified portfolio of stocks. By investing in index funds or ETFs, you can passively earn returns that mirror the performance of the overall market.

Lastly, it's important to have a long-term mindset when investing for passive income. Rome wasn't built in a day, and neither will your passive income empire. Stay disciplined, stick to your investment plan, and let compounding work its magic over time. Remember, investing for passive income is a journey, not a destination.

Investing for passive income is a powerful strategy to achieve financial independence and create a life of abundance. By adopting a frugal lifestyle, diversifying your investments, and focusing on income-generating assets such as dividend stocks, REITs, and index funds, you can steadily build your passive income streams and secure your financial future. A 30 day frugal challenge assist in your investment strategy so you are better able to soend in line with your vision, be mindful and direct any frugal savings to investment opportunities.

Chapter Ten

Maximize your Earning Potential

Maximize your Earning Potential

Maximizing Your Earning Potential

F inancial independence and a life of abundance are not just dreams; they are achievable goals. One of the most effective ways to achieve this is by maximizing your earning potential. You can explore ways to boost your income and create opportunities for financial growth, all while maintaining a frugal lifestyle.

1. Invest in Your Education and Skills: Continuous learning is crucial for personal and professional growth. Take advantage of online courses, workshops, and seminars to enhance your knowledge and skills. By upgrading your qualifications, you increase the likelihood of promotions, salary raises, and better job prospects.

2. Develop a Side Hustle: As outlined above a side hustle not only provides an additional income stream but also offers the opportunity to explore your passions. Whether it's freelancing, tutoring, or starting a small business, find a side gig that aligns with your interests and skills. Remember, even a small endeavor can have a significant impact on your financial well-being.

3. Negotiate Your Salary: When starting a new job or during performance reviews, don't shy away from negotiating your salary. Research industry standards, showcase your accomplishments, and confidently present your case for a higher pay grade. Remember, the worst that can happen is a polite refusal, but you may end up earning more than expected.

4. Leverage the Power of Networking: Building a strong professional network opens doors to new opportunities. Attend industry events, join professional associations, and connect with like-minded individuals. Networking can lead to job referrals, collaborations, and mentorship, ultimately boosting your earning potential.

5. Embrace Entrepreneurship: If you have a brilliant business idea or a product to offer, consider starting your own venture. Entrepreneurship allows you to be your own boss, potentially earn more, and have control over your financial future. However, be prepared for the challenges that come with it and ensure proper planning and execution.

6. Seek Advancement Opportunities: Take on new responsibilities, volunteer for challenging projects, and demonstrate your dedication and commitment at work. By showcasing your potential and willingness to grow, you increase your chances of climbing the corporate ladder and earning a higher income.

Remember, maximizing your earning potential is not just about making more money; it's about creating opportunities for financial growth and achieving a life of abundance. By investing in yourself, exploring side hustles, negotiating salaries, networking, embracing entrepreneurship, and seeking advancement opportunities, you can pave the way for a brighter financial future.

Chapter Eleven

Frugal Shopping and Smart Consumerism

Frugal Shopping and Smart Consumerism

Strategies for Bargain Hunting and Thrift Shopping

I t's easy to feel overwhelmed by the constant urge to spend money in a world where we are constantly bombarded with advertising. But what if there was a way to satisfy your desires without breaking the bank? Bargain hunting and thrift shopping are fantastic strategies that can help you achieve financial independence and live a life of abundance.

One of the most crucial skills in bargain hunting is patience. It's essential to resist the temptation of making impulsive purchases and instead wait for the right moment. Keep an eye on sales, discounts, and promotions. Sign up for newsletters and follow your favorite brands on social media to stay updated on the latest deals. Remember, delayed gratification can lead to significant savings.

Thrift shopping is another fantastic avenue to explore when looking for bargains. Thrift stores, consignment shops, and online marketplaces can be treasure troves for frugal individuals. When thrift shopping, it's essential to have an open mind and a keen eye for quality. Take your time to browse through the racks and shelves, as you never know what hidden gems you might find. Additionally, don't be afraid to negotiate prices, especially at flea markets or yard sales. A polite request for a lower price can often lead to surprising discounts.

Another effective strategy is to embrace the art of couponing. Coupons can provide substantial savings on groceries, household items, and even entertainment. Keep an organized coupon binder or use digital couponing apps to maximize your savings. Combine coupons with sales to enjoy even greater discounts. Just remember to only use coupons for items you genuinely need, as excessive couponing can lead to unnecessary purchases.

Moreover, consider joining online communities and forums dedicated to frugal living and financial independence. These communities are often filled with like-minded individuals who share tips, tricks, and the latest deals they've found. By actively participating in these communities, you can gain valuable insights and stay up to date on the best bargains in town.

Bargain hunting and thrift shopping are not only financially beneficial but also environmentally friendly. By purchasing second-hand items, you reduce waste and contribute to a sustainable lifestyle. So, embrace these strategies, challenge yourself to become a frugal shopper, and watch your savings grow.

To sum up, mastering the art of bargain hunting and thrift shopping is an essential step towards financial independence and a life of abundance. By incorporating these strategies into your daily routine, you can save money, find hidden treasures, and contribute to a more sustainable future.

Making Smart Purchases and Avoiding Impulse Buys

It can be easy to fall into the trap of impulse buying and acting on our emotional impulses. We are constantly bombarded with advertisements and enticing deals that make us feel like we need to buy something right now. However, making smart purchases is crucial for achieving financial independence and living a life of abundance. I

In committing to making smart purchases it is important to understand the difference between needs and wants. Before making any purchase, ask yourself if it is something you truly need or simply something you desire in the moment. By prioritizing your needs over your wants, you can avoid unnecessary spending and focus on building a solid financial foundation.

Another strategy to avoid impulse buying is to create a budget and stick to it. By setting financial goals and tracking your expenses, you can gain a clear understanding of your spending habits and identify areas where you may be prone to impulsive purchases. Additionally, having a budget allows you to allocate funds towards your financial priorities, such as savings or debt repayment, rather than mindlessly spending on things that won't contribute to your long-term goals. If something won't fit this month's budget but you still want next month, you can re-assess if it fits in the next month's budget to purchase. This delay is useful in avoiding reaction impulse buys and really assessing each purchase.

Research and comparison shopping are also essential when it comes to making smart purchases. Before buying a product or service, take the time to read reviews, compare prices, and evaluate the value it will bring to your life. By doing thorough research, you can ensure that you are getting the best deal possible and making a purchase that aligns with your needs and values.

Lastly, it's important to cultivate a mindset of delayed gratification. Instead of giving in to the impulse of instant gratification, practice patience and wait for the right time to make a purchase. This allows you to evaluate whether the item is truly necessary and gives you the opportunity to find better deals or alternatives.

By following these strategies and being mindful of your spending habits, you can make smart purchases that align with your financial goals and values. Remember, frugality is not about depriving yourself, but rather making intentional choices that bring you closer to financial independence and a life of abundance.

Understanding the True Cost of Ownership

It's often easy to get caught up in the allure of owning the latest gadgets, trendy clothing, and luxurious cars. But have you ever stopped to consider the true cost of ownership? That shiny new item may seem like a great deal at first, but when you factor in all the hidden costs, it may not be such a bargain after all.

Whether you are a personal finance enthusiast, someone on a frugal living journey, or striving for FIRE (Financial Independence, Retire Early), understanding the true cost of ownership is crucial. There are various components that make up the true cost of ownership. It's not just about the upfront price tag; it includes factors such as maintenance, repairs, insurance, and depreciation. By analyzing these costs, you will gain a clearer picture of the long-term financial implications of your purchases.

By making mindful choices and evaluating the true cost of ownership, you can avoid falling into the trap of unnecessary debt and overspending. It is importance to consider alternative options to ownership. Renting, sharing, or borrowing items can often be more cost-effective and sustainable.

Understanding the true cost of ownership is a fundamental principle of frugal living and achieving financial independence. By mastering this concept, you will be empowered to make smarter financial decisions, cultivate a more mindful consumption mindset, and ultimately lead a life of abundance and freedom.

Chapter Twelve

Overcoming Challenges and Staying Motivated

Overcoming Challenges and Staying Motivated

Dealing with Peer Pressure and Social Expectations

In today's consumer-driven society, it can be challenging to stay true to your financial goals and embrace frugal living. Peer pressure and societal expectations often push us to conform to certain spending habits, making it difficult to prioritize our long-term financial well-being. However, with the right mindset and strategies, you can navigate these obstacles and maintain your frugal lifestyle while still enjoying a life of abundance.

One solution to dealing with peer pressure and social expectations is to develop a strong sense of self-awareness. Understand your values, goals, and priorities when it comes to personal finance. By having a clear vision of what you want to achieve, you'll be better equipped to resist external influences that may contradict your frugal living choices.

It's important to remember that frugality doesn't mean deprivation. It's about making conscious choices to spend your money wisely and align your expenses with your values. Communicate your financial goals and intentions with your friends and family. Let them know that you're on a journey towards financial independence and that you may need their support in making frugal choices.

When faced with peer pressure to overspend or engage in expensive activities, learn to say no. It's okay to decline invitations that don't align with your financial goals. Instead, suggest alternative, budget-friendly activities that still allow you to connect with others. By setting boundaries and being assertive, you can maintain your frugal lifestyle without feeling isolated or excluded.

Seek out like-minded individuals who share your passion for personal finance and frugal living. Join online communities, attend local meetups, or start a frugal living challenge with friends or family. Surrounding yourself with people who understand and support your financial goals can provide a valuable support system, making it easier to resist peer pressure and stay motivated on your frugal living journey.

Remember, the key to dealing with peer pressure and social expectations is staying true to yourself. Embrace your frugal lifestyle with confidence and conviction. By prioritizing your financial well-being and aligning your expenses with your values, you can achieve financial independence and enjoy a life of abundance while still maintaining strong relationships and connections with others.

Managing FOMO (Fear of Missing Out)

Similar to social pressures it's easy to fall prey to the fear of missing out, or FOMO as it is commonly known. We are bombarded with images and stories of people living seemingly perfect lives on social media, making us question our own choices and accomplishments. This fear can be particularly damaging when it comes to personal finance and frugal living. However, by understanding and managing FOMO, we can take control of our financial journey and create a life of abundance.

FOMO often stems from a deep-rooted belief that we are not good enough or that our lives are lacking in some way. This can lead us to make impulsive decisions, such as buying unnecessary things or spending beyond our means, just to keep up with others. However, true financial independence and abundance come from aligning our spending with our values and long-term goals.

To overcome FOMO, it's important to first recognize and acknowledge our feelings. Understand that social media often presents a distorted version of reality, and what we see is not always an accurate representation of someone's life. By focusing on our own journey and celebrating our achievements, no matter how small, we can cultivate a sense of contentment and gratitude.

Another effective strategy is to set clear financial goals. By creating a roadmap for our financial future, we can prioritize our spending and make conscious choices that align with our values. This empowers us to say "no" to unnecessary expenses and focus on what truly brings us joy and fulfillment.

Additionally, building a supportive community of like-minded individuals can help us combat FOMO. Surrounding ourselves with people who share our values and understand the importance of frugality can provide the motivation and encouragement we need to stay on track. This can be done through joining online forums, attending local meetups, or even starting a frugal living challenge with friends and family.

Ultimately, managing FOMO is about finding balance and being intentional with our choices. It's about understanding that true abundance comes from living within our means, pursuing our passions, and cultivating meaningful relationships. By embracing frugality and adopting a mindset of abundance, we can achieve financial independence and create a life of true fulfillment and contentment.

Celebrating Milestones and Small Wins

In our journey towards financial independence and a life of abundance, it's essential to celebrate not only the big milestones but also the small wins along the way. These moments of achievement are not only worth acknowledging but can also serve as powerful motivators to keep us on track. Small wins may be money saved, money not spent, items re-used or repaired or even new meal planning recipe's used. It also may be mental breakthrough and mindset shift in how you think about your day to day purchases or spending.

When we embark on a 30-day frugal living challenge, every step we take towards our goal is significant. It could be saving a few dollars on groceries, resisting the temptation to indulge in an impulse purchase, or finding a creative way to repurpose something instead of buying new. These seemingly small actions can accumulate to create significant changes in our financial situation over time.

By celebrating these small wins, we reinforce positive behavior and build momentum. It's important to acknowledge and reward ourselves for our efforts, whether it's treating ourselves to a small indulgence, indulging in a favorite hobby, or simply taking a moment to reflect and appreciate our progress. These celebrations create a positive feedback loop, making it easier to continue practicing frugality and maintaining our financial goals.

Moreover, celebrating milestones is equally important. These are the major achievements we set out to accomplish, such as paying off a debt, reaching a savings goal, or achieving a specific financial milestone. These milestones mark significant progress on our journey towards financial independence and should be recognized and celebrated accordingly. Whether it's hosting a small gathering with loved ones, treating ourselves to a special outing, or simply taking the time to acknowledge our achievement privately, celebrating milestones allows us to savor our success and fuels our motivation to keep going.

Remember, it's not just about the end goal; it's about the journey itself. By celebrating milestones and small wins, we infuse our frugal living challenge with a sense of joy and fulfillment. It becomes more than just a challenge; it becomes a lifestyle that we can enjoy and sustain in the long run. So, let's raise a toast to every dollar saved, every debt paid off, and every step forward on our path to financial independence. Cheers to celebrating milestones and small wins!

Chapter Thirteen

Planning for Long-Term Financial Independence

Planning for Long-Term Financial Independence

Understanding Investment Vehicles and Strategies

A s you start being aware of your budgets, spend and income and your money mindset shifts you may start looking towards your longer term financial plan and freedom strategy. Investing is a crucial aspect of achieving financial independence and building a life of abundance. However, navigating the complex world of investment vehicles and strategies can be overwhelming for many individuals. We touched on some aspects of investing in Chapter 9 in regards to building your income but let's dive a little deeper here.

Before delving into specific investment vehicles, it is essential to grasp the concept of risk and return. Every investment carries a certain level of risk, and understanding this risk is vital in selecting suitable investment options. Additionally, investors must assess their risk tolerance, time horizon, and financial goals to align their investments with their individual circumstances.

One of the most common investment vehicles is the stock market. Stocks represent ownership in a company and can provide significant returns over the long term. However, it is crucial to conduct thorough research and analysis before investing in individual stocks. Alternatively, exchange-traded funds (ETFs) or mutual funds pool money from multiple investors to invest in a diversified portfolio of stocks, bonds, or other assets, reducing the risk associated with individual stock picking.

Another popular investment vehicle is real estate. Real estate investing offers various opportunities, such as rental properties, commercial properties, or real estate investment trusts (REITs). Investing in real estate can provide both rental income and potential appreciation over time, making it an attractive option for long-term investors.

For those looking for more conservative options, bonds can be a suitable investment vehicle. Bonds are debt securities issued by corporations or governments, providing fixed interest payments over a specified period. Bonds are generally considered less volatile than stocks, making them a preferred choice for risk-averse investors.

Understanding investment strategies is equally important as selecting the right investment vehicle. Some common strategies include buy and hold, dollar-cost averaging, and diversification. Buy and hold involves purchasing investments with a long-term mindset, ignoring short-term market fluctuations. Dollar-cost averaging involves investing a fixed amount of money at regular intervals, allowing investors to buy more shares when prices are low. Diversification entails spreading investments across different asset classes to reduce risk.

By comprehending investment vehicles and strategies, individuals can create a well-balanced investment portfolio aligned with their financial goals. It is crucial to continually educate oneself and stay updated with market trends to make informed investment decisions. Remember, investing is a long-term commitment, and patience and discipline are key to achieving financial independence and abundance.

Take the first step towards your financial journey by understanding the world of investment vehicles and strategies. With the right knowledge and mindset, you can pave the way for a secure financial future and live a life of abundance.

Creating a Retirement Plan and Saving for the Future

Whether you dream of traveling the world, starting a passion project, or simply enjoying a worry-free retirement, taking control of your finances is the first step towards achieving those goals. In this section we will outline various strategies and tips to help you create a retirement plan and save for the future.

1. Assess your current financial situation: Before diving into retirement planning, it's crucial to have a clear understanding of your current financial situation. Take a close look at your income, expenses, and debts. This will give you an accurate picture of where you stand and help you set realistic goals.

2. Set SMART goals: Setting Specific, Measurable, Achievable, Relevant, and Time-bound (SMART) goals is key to success in

any endeavor, including retirement planning. Determine how much money you will need for retirement and when you want to retire. This will give you a target to work towards and keep you motivated.

3. Create a budget: Developing a budget is an essential part of any frugal living challenge. It allows you to track your expenses, cut unnecessary costs, and allocate funds towards saving for retirement. Identify areas where you can trim expenses, such as dining out or entertainment, and redirect those funds towards retirement savings.

4. Explore retirement account options: Look into different retirement account options available to you, such as a 401(k), Individual Retirement Account (IRA), or Roth IRA. Understand the tax advantages and contribution limits associated with each account, and choose the one that best suits your needs and goals.

5. Maximize employer contributions: If your employer offers a retirement savings plan with an employer match, make sure to contribute enough to maximize their contribution. This is essentially free money that will significantly boost your retirement savings.

6. Diversify your investments: A well-diversified investment portfolio can help protect your retirement savings from market fluctuations. Consider spreading your investments across different asset classes, such as stocks, bonds, and real estate, to minimize risk and maximize returns.

7. Monitor and adjust your plan: It's important to regularly review and adjust your retirement plan as needed. Life circumstances change, and so should your financial strategy. Keep track of your progress, reassess your goals, and make any necessary modifications to stay on track.

Remember, creating a retirement plan and saving for the future is a marathon, not a sprint. It requires discipline, commitment, and consistency. By following these tips and staying focused on your goals, you can achieve financial independence and enjoy a life of abundance in later years. Start today and take the first step towards securing a bright and prosperous future. There are many facebook groups and reading resources available if you are interesting in taking a more indepth look into this area. It is a great place to start and will open a new world of awareness for you.

Incorporating Frugal Living Principles into Long-Term Wealth Building

When it comes to building long-term wealth, incorporating frugal living principles can be a game-changer. By adopting a frugal mindset, you not only save money in the short term but also set yourself up for financial independence and a life of abundance in the long run.

Here we summarize the actionable steps to take over the course of 30 days. You can spend a month prepping for your 30 day challenge and go in ready to be strictly frugal or you can take a month to chip away and the areas listed. Your 30 day challenge is your own but I recommend doing a 30 day frugal living challenge and least twice a year to reset those automatic habits you fall into and really be able to evaluate your mindset and daily habits to align with your longer term financial freedom and abundance plan.

Day 1: Assess Your Spending Habits
Start by evaluating your current spending habits. Identify areas where you tend to overspend and make a conscious effort to cut back. This could include reducing dining out expenses, canceling unnecessary subscriptions, or finding ways to save on utilities.

Day 5: Create a Budget
Developing a budget is crucial for tracking your expenses and ensuring you stay on track with your financial goals. Learn how to create a

comprehensive budget that allows for savings and investment contributions.

Day 10: Embrace Minimalism

Declutter your life and adopt a minimalist approach to possessions. By simplifying your lifestyle, you reduce the desire for material possessions, freeing up both physical and mental space for more meaningful experiences.

Day 15: DIY and Repurposing

Discover the joy of do-it-yourself projects and repurposing items. Learn how to mend clothes, repair household items, and repurpose old furniture. Not only will you save money, but you will also develop valuable skills along the way.

Day 20: Meal Planning and Cooking at Home

Save money on groceries by planning your meals in advance and cooking at home. Explore frugal recipes, meal prepping tips, and incorporate more plant-based options into your diet. Batch cook and freeze food for easy meals and set up an easy meal plan that works for you.

Day 25: Negotiate and Seek Deals

Develop your negotiation skills and become a savvy shopper. Learn how to find the best deals, negotiate prices, and take advantage of discounts and coupons.

Day 30: Automate Savings and Investments

Finally, automate your savings and investment contributions. Set up automatic transfers to your savings account and establish regular investments in low-cost index funds. By making saving and investing a priority, you ensure that your wealth-building journey continues even when life gets busy.

Incorporating frugal living principles into your long-term wealth-building strategy is a powerful way to achieve financial independence and unlock a life of abundance. By following this 30-day challenge, you will develop new habits that will serve you well for years to come. Remember, building wealth is a marathon, not a sprint, and embracing frugality is a key ingredient for success.

Chapter Fourteen

Enjoy Ever Increasing Abundance

Your Journey to Financial Independence and Abundance

C ongratulations! You have completed the 30-day frugal living challenge and taken a significant step towards financial independence and a life of abundance. Throughout this book, we have explored various strategies and techniques to help you achieve your financial goals while embracing the principles of frugal living. Now, it's time to reflect on your journey and set your sights on a future filled with financial freedom.

By implementing the frugal living principles outlined in this book, you have learned to prioritize your spending, cut unnecessary expenses, and make conscious choices about how you use your money. You have witnessed firsthand the power of small changes in your daily habits, which can have a profound impact on your financial well-being in the long run.

Remember, financial independence is not just about accumulating wealth; it's about gaining control over your finances and living a life that aligns with your values and aspirations. As you move forward, keep these key takeaways in mind:

1. Mindful Spending: We have emphasized the importance of mindful spending throughout this book. By being intentional about where your money goes, you can ensure that your resources are directed towards things that truly matter to you.

2. Embracing Minimalism: Living a frugal lifestyle often goes hand in hand with embracing minimalism. By decluttering your life and letting go of excessive material possessions, you can create space for what truly brings you joy and fulfillment.

3. Saving and Investing: Frugality should not be limited to cutting expenses. It's equally important to save and invest wisely. Set aside a portion of your income for emergencies, and explore investment options that align with your goals and risk tolerance.

4. Financial Independence Retire Early (FIRE): The concept of FIRE has gained popularity in recent years, and it aligns closely with the principles discussed in this book. Achieving financial independence and retiring early is within your reach if you continue to prioritize frugality and make smart financial decisions.

As you embark on your journey towards financial independence and abundance, remember that it is a marathon, not a sprint. Be patient with yourself and celebrate each small victory along the way. Surround yourself with like-minded individuals who share your goals and can provide support and encouragement.

Lastly, never forget that financial independence is not an end in itself, but a means to live a life that truly fulfills you. Use your newfound financial freedom to pursue your passions, spend time with loved ones, and make a positive impact on the world around you.

Thank you for joining us on this transformative 30-day journey towards financial independence and a life of abundance. We wish you all the best in your continued pursuit of financial freedom and a future filled with endless possibilities.

If you enjoyed this book it really helps that you give us an amazon review! Also check out some of the other titles in our 30 day Challenge series